Silhouettes, How to Cut

This revised printing in 2007, has comments of REVIEWERS and PAPERCUTTERS *who know what Silhouette Cutting for Fun and Money* is about, and we continually receive letters of appreciation for what the past six printings have done for others.

"At last! A handbook stuffed with essential information on how to practice, find supplies, and keep the rare art/craft of "miniature" silhouettes alive."
Guild of American Papercutters

"You've made a great contribution to all who catch the silhouette fever."
Papercutting World

"Imagine my surprise when I bought your book. I can't draw a straight line, but scissors did the trick. Look where it got me."
J. Jones, now cutting at Disney World

Profile Press
6051 Greenway Court
Manassas, VA 20112

www.profilepress.org
profilepress@comcast.net

D1114559

Silhouette Cutting, for Fun and Money

$$

Published by: Profile Press
                  6051 Greenway Court
                  Manassas, VA 20112

                  www.profilepress.org
                  profilepress@comcast.net

                  Printed: 1987, 1990, 1995, 2004, 2007
                  Revised: 2007

                  Ann Woodward, Author
                  Deidre Woodward, Graphic Designer
                  Ray Woodward, Jr., Editorial Assistant

Although the authors and publisher have exhaustively researched all sources to ensure the accuracy and completeness of the information contained in this book, we assume no responsibility for errors, inaccuracies, omissions or any other inconsistency herein. Any slights against people or organizations are not intentional. Readers should consult an accountant on specific application to their individual publishing ventures.

WOODWARD, Ann and Deidre
    Silhouette Cutting for Fun and Money

    1. Self-publishing -Handbooks, manuals, etc.

LC 87-90602

Contents

Dedication:

This book is dedicated to the thousands who have asked: "How did you learn to cut silhouettes?"

But, most of all, it is dedicated to the many people who yearn for a challenging, exciting hobby or profession in this "little known" art or craft that holds the fascination of a Mona Lisa.

We hope this book helps you reach the widest possible audience and pass on a legacy that will be handed down from one generation to the next so that the fine art of silhouette-cutting will never become a lost art.

If your Mother told you to find a subject few had touched, and master it, this could be it. It will keep you busy and open a brand new world to **Fun and Money.**

Practice, practice, practice! Take your time and do it right, and enjoy, enjoy, enjoy! That's the best advice we can give you.

Acknowledgment:

We are grateful:

First, for our introduction to silhouette-cutting -- observing a free-hand cutter who left us spellbound with the results of her "magic scissors" at a shopping mall;

Second, for the thousands of inquiries as to how to get started in this fascinating and lucrative business;

Third, to those who helped us relate, with simplicity, "everything you need to know to cut silhouettes for recreation, relaxation, gratification, fun and money." They were:

Delores Coker, who contributed to Library of Congress research,

Deidre Woodward, who did the graphics, typesetting, and co-authored,

Margaret Thompson, Technical

Ray Woodward, Jr., the consulting editor who smoothed our pathways and made it all a pleasant undertaking.

but most importantly, we give Praise to God who gave us thoughts that convey our message to you.

Preface:

This book is intended as a history (to enlighten your clients), laced with instruction on *Silhouette Cutting for Fun and Money.*

Preparation of the book involved intense research at the Library of Congress as well as a nation-wide survey of silhouette-cutters. The author also traveled from Coast to Coast and in Europe to learn from the few remaining professional silhouette artists the mystique of this little known craft/art.

Our accomplishments are a result of determination and experience. If the light we have shed on silhouette cutting paves the way for you to learn this rewarding art, our efforts will not have been in vain.

This revised book is the 7th printing since 1987. We have added many silhouette artists to the market, yet, there is room for more in our 300 million population. Is there a silhouette artist in your community? If you don't want to earn extra income, there are many other remunerations, as we have learned from the many glowing letters we have received.

What is a Silhouette?

A shadow, frozen in time and space, for future generations to ponder: "What was it like in those times? If it could speak - - what would it say?"

The mystery lingers on like a Mona Lisa in profile.

Ann Woodward
1987

Introduction:

We wrote this book because:

1. SILHOUETTE-CUTTING WAS A "DYING" ART or CRAFT - whichever you choose to call it. In 1987, when the book was first published, we located less than 25 "professional" silhouette cutters in the United States, with the exception of those at Disney World and Disneyland.

Many people are unfamiliar with silhouettes and can't appreciate their value. Others are desperately looking for a silhouette artist because they possess some that have been handed down from one generation to the next and they want to continue the tradition. Silhouettes are a collector's item and old silhouettes demand a price at antique shows.

It is discouraging to search for a Silhouette Artist when you need one for a particular occasion, and there's none to be found. Since our book was first published, many people have learned to cut silhouettes, as a hobby or business, but there's room for more. Every community or at least a metropolitan area, should have one for the many opportunities offered.

2. To Acquire information on **How To Cut Silhouettes** is very difficult. Some silhouette cutters lead one to believe it to be a "mysterious" ability few possess. One prominent artist stated:

"Dissemination of the knowledge of cutting silhouettes will remain fairly closely guarded. Beyond

the knowledge of how to cut them is the source of proper paper, the best glue and how to use it, proper mounting, good location and marketing. I do not know of any intelligent Artist who would assist you in the preparation of a book that would contain the seeds of their own economic demise."

This statement gave us determination to seek pertinent information and devise a simple method to **Learn How To Practice** and become a professional silhouette cutter. There is a great deal of information on the history of silhouettes, but the 15 silhouette cutters who responded to our survey, had no suggestions on a technique that would teach one to cut. Some of them implied that it was a "gift" or that it would take years of study in the field of art. (*To our knowledge, there is no art school that teaches Silhouette-Cutting.*)

We taught ourselves and this book explains how you, too, can learn to cut. We could not let 20 years of untold benefits go by without sharing this with others who are caught up in the spell of the "magic" scissors.

You will practice this technique on your friends and soon start to spread your wings. This book contains all the information you need to know to get started and do business. If you can follow lines and a pattern, you can learn to cut silhouettes. It offers hours of peaceful recreation and the pleasure of accomplishment. When a profile emerges from a simple piece of paper, it brings many remunerations as well as fun and money.

Psychologists and educators have recognized it as powerful in concentration and following directions.

It demands close attention without frustration, also promotes dexterity of fingers and aids in therapy.

Many therapists use this book to help their clients. (When one is cutting silhouettes, he is not thinking or worrying about anything else).

You will find the history interesting, the suggestions invaluable and locating the supplies most helpful. More that that, you will experience all we have said and done and in days to come you will feel like you've known how to cut silhouettes forever. You'll find that it is amazing what one can do -- with scissors, paper and glue.

You didn't know that it was in you. Today you are a silhouette cutter. Tomorrow you are a professional Silhouette Artist. So, here's to your success. It's a lot more simple than you think, and it will open a brand new interesting world. It took a long time for us to discover, so don't YOU keep waiting.

Jewish Cut-Out

Polish Paper Cut-Out By Roma Starczewska

German Silhouette

You will want to know something of the history of paper-cutting as it evolved into forms of craft/art. The curiosity and fascination of your clients prompt many questions. The following will give you some idea of this ancient art, but much more can be learned in libraries.

Paper was developed in China about 2000 years ago, and the first results of paper-cutting are shown in family seals used to identify property. Later known as "Monikiri," it was used for designs on textiles. Knives were used first to cut the paper, but shortly thereafter scissors were invented, offering greater precision in preparing intricate paper cutouts. Shadow puppets emerged from cutting and their popularity spread into India and Indonesia. The art and craft traveled to other countries and developed in different ways to serve the imagination and culture practices of diverse nationalities.

Craft guilds in Turkey, in the 16th Century made carved works of paper with knives, not scissors. Later on these were adapted for adorning furniture and household utensils.

The Jewish art of paper-cutting can be traced to the 17th Century in North Africa and Europe. Scribes, teachers and students cut out intricate designs to mark the direction of Jerusalem. Today, many Jewish families do paper-cuts for holidays and festive occasions.

In Poland, children were kept busy on long winter evenings, by doing "Wycinanki" (vi-chee-non-ki). These were designs of stars, animals, butterflies, birds and flowers, cut out in multiple quantities from folded sheets of paper, with sheep shears. (If you did a similar thing by folding and making a chain of children holding hands, when you were a child, imagine how cumbersome it would have been to use sheep shears.) The Polish people added color to their paper, and the white-washed homes had a fresh, look by the time Spring arrived.

In Germany, paper-cutting was called "Scherenschnitte" (shear-enschnit-tah). This means "snip with scissors." There, it emerged from a primitive art form to more detail, such as delicate wings of a butterfly, leaves of grass, individual feathers of a bird, etc. Many old German designs have been reproduced. Instead of cutting multiple designs, as in Poland, the Scherenschnitte artist today simply reproduces (by drawing or tracing a scene) on the reverse side of silhouette paper, then begins by cutting the most intricate interior parts first, leaving certain connecting parts until later. For your information, small designs can be anchored on a board for easy handling, while a larger design can be rolled on an empty paper towel tube and unrolled as it is being cut.

Mexico offers beautiful tissue paper-cuttings, known as "Papel Picado." A style of its own, with its array of colors, the flowers and "piñatas" are most attractive.

In France, paper-cutting was done for the production of shadow plays, but we think of Paris as the birthplace of the "Silhouette." If you go there today, one of the many artists may be trailing you and cutting your silhouette at the same time. While he may be able to capture "likeness" in this manner, it is only at eye level that one can capture a true likeness.

In Great Britain and the United States, paper-cutting of people's profiles has been called "shades" and "shadows" as well as "silhouettes."

Although paper-cutting dates back to the time when paper was first invented, it has not lost it's charm. Think of Henri Matisse, in his final days. After exploring many other forms of art, when he could no longer hold his paint brush, he discovered the beauty of paper-cutting. When these works were first shown in Paris in 1949, it was as if painting itself had been reborn. He used vibrant colors and brought out ideas that didn't suit for easel painting, sculpture, or drawing in pencil and ink. They were ideas whose time had come, and they proved that paper-cutting art can be equally as beautiful as any other form of art.

Matisse's paper cut-out of WILD POPPIES – with vivid colors and fanciful shapes.

Chinese Seal

Greek Vase

Egyptian wall-hanging

Silhouette, 500 B.C., France

Motion Picture Silhouettes

History of Silhouette Art:

2

Silhouette art was first exhibited on the walls of limestone caves in France, Spain, South Africa, Australia and elsewhere, more than 20 or 30 thousand years ago. During the stone age, before man had the skill to domesticate animals or develop tools, he had the facility to graphically express, in a two-dimensional art form, his thoughts, dreams, superstitions and creatures of the environment. Outlines of the buffalo, bear, fox, wolves, sprinting people and human hands were done in profile in charcoal.

As early as 6,000 years ago the progress of man was represented by silhouettes in Egyptian tombs and temples. There, we find scenes of daily activities, battles, death and burial rituals. Expressions of life emerged much later on Greek pottery, showing bridal scenes, music lessons and various sports being performed 2,000 years ago. Were it not for these silhouettes, the progress of early mankind would not be displayed.

Silhouettes took precedence over the other art forms because of their ability to communicate quickly on a basic level. That same reasoning applies today through many illustrations -- advertisements in business, entertainment, sports and other areas such as road signs and subjects that cross language barriers.

Did you think the popularity of silhouettes originated in Paris? Actually, "silhouette" is a French word named after Monsieur Etienne de Silhouette (1709-1767), the Minister of Finance who did this form of paper-cutting as a hobby.

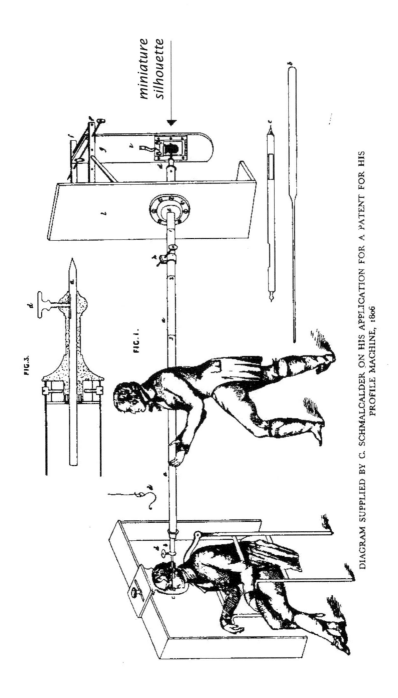

miniature silhouette

FIG.3.

FIG.1.

DIAGRAM SUPPLIED BY C. SCHMALCALDER ON HIS APPLICATION FOR A PATENT FOR HIS PROFILE MACHINE, 1806

16

17th to mid-19th Century

Although silhouette art exhisted from the earliest of time, its popularity was greatest between the 17th and mid-19th Century. Shadows, sketches, and mechanical apparatuse were the techniques used in creating the profile.

In the 1800's, Charles Wilson Peale, at his museum in Philadelphia, used the physiognotrace for making his "hollow cuts." A hollow cut is what is left after the inner profile is lifted. Black cloth or paper was placed behind the hollow cut to produce one silhouette, and the inner profile was matted to make a second silhouette. Both silhouettes are rarely done today as it is an exceptional silhouette-cutter who can maintain both the inside and outside of the cut in perfect condition for two silhouettes.

The physiognotrace had a device that was fastened to the wall. The sitter placed his head against a hollow plaque for steadiness and then a brass gnomon was run over the head. Arms, operating on a pantograph principle, traced the head's outline on paper in a smaller size, with point. Scissors were then used to cut within that line to make the hollow cut and the silhouette.

In 1631, the pantograph was invented. This was used to reduce the size of a profile. Soon afterwards, "miniature" silhouettes were used to decorate snuff boxes, cameos, and other items.

John Casper Lavatar, who lived from 1741 to 1801, made use of the LIMOMACHIA for the purpose of creating a profile. This was used to explain his theory that characters and mental attitudes could be discerned by facial features. He collected more physionomical knowledge from silhouettes than any other kind of portrait. This led to psyco-analysis. He had this to say about the profile in silhouette: "Pride and humility are more prominent than vanity in "shades." Natural benevolence, internal power, flexibility, peculiar sensibility, and especially infantile innocence are expressed; great under- standing, rather than stupidity, profound thought much better than clearness of conception; creative powers rather than acquired knowledge, especially in the outline of the forehead and eye bones."

In our instructions for cutting, we point out some of Lavatar's observations of the profiles made from his physiognotrace.

Through the years, several machines were invented to produce a silhouette, and some artists painted them on porcelain or glass. However, it was not until August Edouart, in England, took a pair of scissors and cut freehand (without first sketching) that silhouette-cutting became a real art. Before then, silhouettes lacked the look of a precision cut.

While Edouart was in America, 1826-1836, others learned his simplified way of cutting silhouettes. Itinerant silhouette-cutters roamed the countryside and found it quite profitable until the camera was invented. By 1850, most of them had vanished, along with the secrets of their trade. Today, many of the silhouettes that Edouart had cut have been handed down for us to observe at The National Portrait Gallery in Washington, D.C.

Self-Portrait of August Edouart, the foremost "free-hand" artist.
By 1828 he was supreme master of this art.

Courtesy of Bernard Nevill Jackson, New York

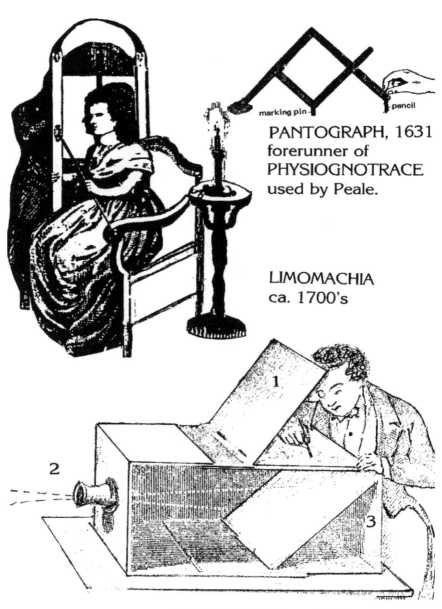

PANTOGRAPH, 1631
forerunner of
PHYSIOGNOTRACE
used by Peale.

marking pin

pencil

LIMOMACHIA
ca. 1700's

CAMERA OBSCURA ca. 1700's
Thomas Jefferson brought one from France.

One of the most outstanding artist was William Henry Brown of South Carolina. He could meet a person then cut his silhouette by memory the following day.

Popularity of the silhouette extended beyond distinguished citizens and families. We discovered the year book for 1840 at the University of Pennsylvania carried the entire graduation class in individual silhouettes.

The silhouette was often referred to as a "cheap likeness," but it served a real purpose for those who could not afford the time or money for a portrait. Today, it is a treasure for those who now have them as family heirlooms.

If you were a sketch artist, you would first draw the profile, then cut. When you have several waiting clients, you will be glad you learned to do as Edouart did -- just observe and begin cutting without leaning on an art background. (Thanks to Leonardo da Vincia and Lavatar who figured out God's proportions for fashioning mankind, you can rely on these measurements for determining for almost every profile). This is the method you will learn by following the instructions in this handbook. All you need is paper, glue, and a pair of good scissors. You don't have be an artist, or know how to draw. But, you'll learn to cut free-hand which takes much less time. Believe it or not, you'll be doing it in five minutes in three months! Want to bet?

Silhouette Cutting Today

There are three methods currently used to create a profile:

1.   Trace a shadow and produce a large profile. This can be reduced to miniature by use of a grid or a Xerox reduction process.

2.   Sketch a person's profile before cutting it, which requires art experience.

3.   Observe and cut free-hand, by using the scissors instead of a sketch pencil. The first two methods take considerable time and do not hold the intrigue and interest of a free-hand silhouette. (To do this, you may need to practice on patterns as well as study the proportions.)

The above techniques for cutting silhouettes have served a purpose in capturing a likeness that can be treasured through the years, and can be considered a work of art. Before the arrival of the camera, many who could not afford a portrait, availed themselves of this "'cheap" likeness that recorded their image and is now a prized possession and a family heirloom.

In your school years, perhaps your used the 1st means of making your likeness. Have you a large silhouette done in this manner? Silhouettes such as these can hold many memories, but are seldom displayed. Mothers prefer miniature silhouettes rather than a large one traced from a shadow.

Some teachers still cut silhouettes by projecting a shadow on the wall. Many would relinquish this task if they could find a silhouette-cutter. (This is where you can HAVE FUN and MONEY.)

In addition, to paper, glue and scissors, you'll need two things:

First, *models*. That's easy. You will find them at the swimming pool, school outings, Girl Scouts, parties, etc.

Second, *confidence*. Relax your wrists and have no qualms about what comes forth from your "magic" scissors. With practice, from sample patterns that instill observation and concentration, you'll soon get the knack of it. You'll gain confidence before you realize it.

As you can surmise, from the various methods employed by other silhouette-cutters, the object is to obtain a likeness, regardless of the method used. If that is achieved in the eyes of the beholder, you have accomplished your mission regardless of your technique.

Sample Holiday Card

(fold)

- -

We got our heads together to
WISH YOU A MERRY CHRISTMAS
Mary, John, Jane, Kit, Joe
1986

3

Who Wants A Silhouette?

Out of almost 300 million people in our country, and nearly eight million babies added each year, do you doubt that *You* could keep busy cutting silhouettes for **FUN and MONEY**? There's Valentine's Day, Spring Fling, Mother's Day, Father's Day, or Any Day to gladden a heart with a silhouette. Schedule appointments for these occasions several weeks in advance. In the fall, there will be so many festivals that you will want to pick the best of several events for the few week-ends remaining for Holiday gifts. Weekdays you will cut at schools as a convenience to mothers.

Who wants to wait for another picture as a gift when it takes only 5 minutes to have a lovely silhouette? Pictures come and go but nobody throws away a silhouette. People who appreciate art know the value of a silhouette. You will find them in the most sophisticated interior designs and they never go out of style. Perhaps you have the memory of one that hung for years in a home and its beauty and mystery lingers on. Once you are known as a silhouette cutter, your life will never be the same. When you begin cutting at bazaars, fairs, and elsewhere, you will attract crowds. Many people will wonder what it is all about, seeing people crowded around someone sitting in a chair.

Most people have never seen a miniature silhouette artist. Some are too embarrassed to ask what is going on as they observe you. When they pause, they will hear you telling the history of silhouettes and will believe that you possess "magic scissors." After you show the audience the "likeness" which emerges from the paper, very few can resist sitting for a silhouette. A few may pass on and "think about it" and later you'll hear from them. It's just something they can't put out of their minds.

Silhouette artists are a rarity and when people see a silhouette being cut, they want to have it done. Otherwise when would they have another opportunity unless they went to Disney World or Disneyland where it is available.

Now You Ask: "So You Think I Can Learn?"

You've read some of the history, have seen a few samples of silhouettes, and you've caught the "fever." You'll never be the same again!

You learned how some of our 17th and 18th Century artist cut with machines or by sketching, but you'll find it much easier to learn how to cut free-hand. Practice with typewriter paper, brown paper sacks or any other kind of paper that offers sufficient texture and weight. If you use black paper, have white paper in front of it to avoid eye strain. (Silhouette paper is folded so that the black is always inside and the white outside.)

You'll be surprised how easy it is to cut silhouettes. Instead of using the patterns for practice and confidence, you may want to "let go" and cut free-hand from the beginning.

Your first silhouettes of this action may turn out to be caricatures, but this is not a bad fault if you have achieved any degree of likeness. Cutting caricatures, which some silhouette-cutters emphasize, is a study in character and excellent practice in speed. As you advance, caricature cuts help to attain perfection in catching a likeness with the scissors.

"Will I Be Nervous?"

Not if you've practiced with family and friends and have learned about perspective. When you "spread wings" after practicing on patterns for several weeks, you'll be so busy concentrating on your subject that you'll forget your nervousness.

You can turn any idle moment into practice, either by using the patterns herein, or just making ripples, stops, and turns with scissors and paper. This could take the place of knitting while you are watching TV, listening to music, or chatting with a friend. While you are gaining this experience, you are warding off arthritis by relaxing and exercising those fingers and wrists.

If you have run out of things to entertain children, this would be the very thing to teach them dexterity and concentration, which could be meaningful for the rest of their lives, and even a source of income for college.

If you stop and think of the many opportunities you will not want to waste any time in learning *Silhouette Cutting for Fun and Money.* This may be the very thing you need to earn Social Security and to contribute to IRA and Keogh Plan.

There is a powerful stimulus in having someone look up to you in awe and watch you perform with those "magic scissors."

As you exhibit at Shows and rub elbows with others, you will gain additional insight into this art as well as great respect from others. (Clients for silhouettes appreciate all the fine arts and are delighted there is someone to offer them this form of art.)

Silhouette Gift Cards. In making two, fold and cut. Mat on folded cardboard.

fold

You may have a better start without knowledge of art. There will be no "hang ups" with sketching because you simply begin by letting your scissors do the work, instead of having to first block and plan, as the artist does. Scissor-cutting comes very easily for most people who try it.

Have your scissors and paper handy and catch a minute whenever you can to wiggle your hands and practice. This may be while you are waiting for someone, traveling, or relaxing at the swimming pool. If you have no model around, use a profile pattern for practice. You should get the "hang of it" in a short time and after that your opportunities are unlimited.

This simplified book and scissors, paper, and glue will get you started. When you go "professional" you need only to add table, chair, business cards and some really good "iris" surgical scissors, silhouette paper and some advertising. This book will not go out of date. It will be timely 100 years from now, and the silhouettes you produce will probably be around for the next 100 years, too.

Pictures come and go, but nobody throws away a silhouette. That is why every customer should write his name and birth date on the silhouette you cut and mat. Had this been done on some of the silhouettes we possess, we would be very pleased. The date "1832" on a scrap of paper found with a bundle of silhouettes in the attic of a home being restored is the only clue toward believing they could have been done by Peale's physiognatrace.

Silhouettes are the simplest, easiest, quickest and cheapest method of portraiture.

Simple, because there are no lights nor shadows; the sole appeal is outline.

Easy, because, with the scissors and paper you can see a line before you make it. Also, you have your work and your model up on the same plane and are less apt to lose perspective than when, in drawing, you look at your model on a plane and then proceed to put what you see on paper.

Quick, because it is possible to cut a silhouette outline in less than a minute.

Inexpensive, because the cost of the paper is so little (about 2 cents for a silhouette.)

Where Do I Begin?

First, you will want to practice. Shake your wrist so that it is limber, then relax and warm up your fingers by getting out your scissors (embroidery scissors will do, to begin). Take a large sheet of paper such as typing, scratch, or wrapping paper. Cut to 4"x6" size and fold over. Instead of letting the scissors cut around the paper, feed the paper into the scissors with your non-dominant hand as long as necessary before the "stop." The scissors should rest comfortably in the dominant thumb and middle finger. (Some may prefer the ring finger – it's a matter of which you find most natural.) The non-dominant thumb and forefinger presses the front of the fold. The silhouette scissors must have a sharp point.

We will now practice **Features Found in Silhouette Cutting:**

1.   Straight cut: Clamp down with your scissors and cut to the end of the blade. That didn't give you any trouble. Now, lets try fancy cuts.

2.   Wave cut: Move the paper evenly with scissors, from side to side while cutting (Use this under the chin, on the forehead or the hair line.)

3.   Scallop cut: A combination of the "wave cut" and "stop", cut into the paper, then swing the paper methodically while cutting, and "stop", repeat. (Use this for ruffles, hair line and slicing inside silhouette.)

4.   Stop: A direct turn of the paper in the scissors, so that the resulting line is at angle with the one preceeding. Take a new start with the paper, turn the paper and cut again. You have observed the "stop", (Used at the throat, lip line, nostril, eyelash, and nape of neck.)

5.   Pulled edge: Pull paper through scissors while making cuts. The paper is torn irregularly between each cut. Any degree of irregularity can be achieved. (Used for irregular hair lines, bangs, mustache, and beard.)

6.   Feather edge: Paper is shaved with tip of scissors. You can make as much as 120 cuts to an inch. (Used for cowlicks, cropped hair, feathers, and furs.) Cuts are made with tips of scissors snipping inward.

7.   Eyelet: Dig the sharp tip into the paper and whirl it around, cutting out a circle. The way you whirl the paper determines the size of the eyelet. (Used for buttons, earrings, bows, and barrettes.)

8.   Inside line cutouts:

Glasses - as you reach the bridge of the nose, observe the design of the glasses. When you have cut the outline of the glasses, turn the silhouette upside down toward you and cut straight down (comparing the distance to the nostril) then curve up to the right, making a half tear-drop effect leaving a sliver of paper to show the glasses. Next, turn silhouette face up again. Be careful not to snip the top of glasses as you cut a narrow strip toward the ear to indicate the strut.

Necklines - cut a fine line from nape of neck to front, then cut UP and make a V, or curve the scissors UP to make it oval.

Man's Collar - cut from nape of neck, maybe make a V, then cut DOWN for wing tip and back to the nape. Add a coat in the same manner, showing the lapel. If a tie protrudes near the knot, cut IN to show the light.

Hair - this can be a distinctive part. Observe length, shape, texture and style. Show highlights by making incisions then cutting slits here and there.

Pigtails - this depends where they are placed. If they appear on the side of the head, cut outs will be necessary to accentuate them. If they are long and hang down over the shoulder, you may not have to cut into the head. If you explain the circumstances client may change her mind and select another style.

Pony tails - is there a space between the pony tail and back of the head? Does it need a gap? If so, make an incision for the gap, then close it.

Bangs and Short Hair - can make a fine hairline cut. May need feathering. (This can distinguish a girl from a boy.)

Curls - follow the outline and wiggle your scissors. A cut inside with a small slice at the scallop will accentuate the curl.

Cowlicks - they hold special memories at the crown or forehead. (Use the feather edge with a twist.)

Waves - on the face, make a thin cut and let the light shine through.

Cropped - pull or feather edge and rub finger across to make it stand up.

Straight - try to distinguish it with a flip or slight wave to show bulk. It maybe necessary to put a bow or barrette on the profile to distinguish a girl from a boy.

Bows - cut them attached to head or neck then embellish them with cut outs.

Some people prefer not to have that embellishment. It takes more time. If you have a waiting line, try skipping it. (Every minute means dollars!) On the other hand, it pays to keep someone sitting in the chair to attract others, and the longer you keep that person there, promotes advertising. That's why it is nice to chat about the history of silhouettes or get to know your customer. (At fairs, bazaars, etc, we've met the most interesting people from all walks of life who have stopped to relax and have their silhouette done.)

Detail can depict character and make for a more distinctive silhouette, but it leaves less to the imagination.

Features Found in Silhouette Cutting

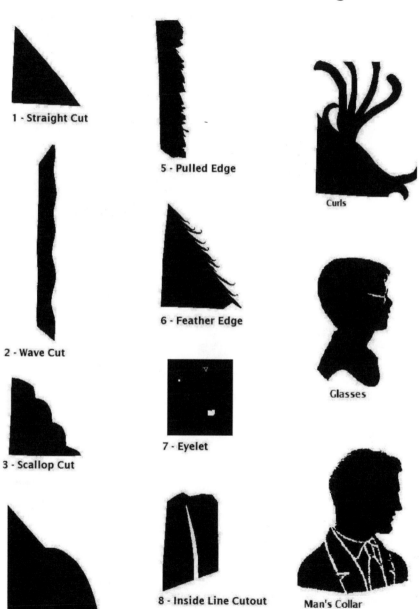

1 - Straight Cut

2 - Wave Cut

3 - Scallop Cut

4 - Stop

5 - Pulled Edge

6 - Feather Edge

7 - Eyelet

8 - Inside Line Cutout

Curls

Glasses

Man's Collar

Is it a vase? Look at the space.
You guessed it. There's a face or two. See?

Did you do this in school? YOU CAN CUT.

Unknown Russian Artist, 1816.

Study the proportions and think of them as you cut. Soon, you will be able to observe the angles, lines, and spaces, as well as negative space around the profile. These lines and spaces can be projecting, retreating, straight, flexible, arched, broken, angular, etc. You will OBSERVE as you cut upward; whether it be from the left or right side of the profile.

You will note where one line ends (which means "stop") and another begins. The lines lie at certain angles in relation to each other, with curved lines fitting into certain spaces. In your deep concentration you forget you are looking at a face you are merely looking at lines, curves, angles and shapes.

As you read instructions, look at sample silhouette patterns. If the PROPORTIONS of the profile confuse you, begin by making copies of the silhouette patterns and practice cutting them with a relaxed wrist. As you study these patterns for different age groups, the proportions as outlined by Lavatar in the 1700's and Leonardo Vinci will be recognized and our explanation will be understood. Of course there are exceptions to the rule on determining proportions, but we have found very few. Some individuals have more chin, nose, forehead, and hair, and the need for orthodontistry may alter some patterns. However, when the silhouette has been cut and you give it the "one-eye" test, in cases a mere snip here and there can turn it into a "likeness." (See p. 43)

We do not know if other gave thought to the principles of Lavatar or Leonardo de Vinci as they simply don't discuss "how to cut" silhouettes. We know this technique works with but few exceptions, as you will find out when you begin observing and cutting.

Learning Proportions

Fold your paper to be 3 ¼" wide and 4" tall. This is the size you will normally use in cutting a "miniature." Smaller, would not be as relaxing to the hands. For some adults, make the size larger.

Next, sit about 4 feet from the client, at eye-level. A child will need a higher seat to be seen at this level. Direct your gaze at first to the negative space around the head. You will see that space as a shape. It is like doing a dance, imagining your scissors going around the form. Cut large at first, as it is easier to observe every detail of the outline.

If you are right handed, client's profile should be facing right, and you begin cutting the silhouette paper at the lower right hand corner from bottom to top. Left-handed cutters may find it more comfortable to begin from bottom of the lower left corner and cut up on the left side.

CHEST comes first, then start viewing the **NECK**. Is it a swan neck that does not demand a cover-up collar? Would the person look better in frills, bow tie, or is there an Adam's Apple? *STOP* and observe.

UNDER CHIN - full, determined, double or sharp? (From the time you begin until you finish the silhouette, the under-chin may change, (particularly with children), a snip or two after the "one-eye" test can make the adjustment.)

THROAT to CHIN - Is there a scallop?
CHIN-pointed, curved, or protruded? Small children may have chin protruding as far as lips and nose. In adults: **CHIN to EYE** equals **EYE** to top of **SKULL**. **CHIN to NOSTRIL** is 1/3rd; **NOSTRIL to EYEBROW** is 1/3rd. (The shape varies.) **EYEBROW to FOREHEAD** – is 1/3rd. **CHIN to MOUTH** equals **THROAT to CHIN,** normally. Is it a "turkey throat" or a "double-chin"?

    CHIN to BOTTOM of LIP equals **BOTTOM of LIP** to **NOSTRIL.** Dip the lip in slightly. (Teeth do not look good in a silhouette so don't have mouth open.) Definitely *STOP* here with scissors and observe **UPPER LIP.** Does it curve slightly toward the nose or is it straight? *This feature gives emphasis to a silhouette.*

    MOUTH LINE - 2/3d's up from **CHIN to NOSTRIL** -its shape varies. Is it straight, curved, or puckered?

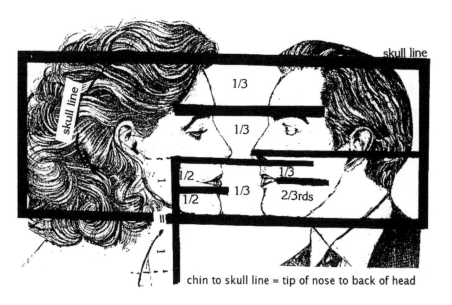

chin to skull line = tip of nose to back of head

NOSE - Be sure to observe the lower line of the nose. Does it go down or turn up? From **NOSE** to its **BRIDGE** is it Roman, pug, or is there a bump somewhere? The outer contour of the tip of the **NOSE, UPPER LIP, LOWER LIP and CHIN** often fall on a slanted line. Observe the length of the **NOSE** in comparison to the length of the chin. Just above **BRIDGE of NOSE** is where eyelash protrudes.

EYELASH - either cut a curve or ink it on. (Some artists don't give eyelashes to the male. We think they are needed to show distinction.) If client wears GLASSES, ignore the eyelashes. (See p. 36)

BROW and FOREHEAD - Is there an arch in the brow? Does it slant or curve? Will you cover it with hair?

HAIRLINE – *STOP* with the scissors when you reach the hairline, then do what the hair dictates until you are a little past top center where the head usually peaks. Then you will turn to the back side to cut. Now you are half-finished.

BACK SIDE – You can either get up and go around the other side of the client and cut, or slide your scissors to the opposite side and cut until you reach the top of the head. The back of head usually gives more problems than the front, especially boys. The nape of the neck is at a level half-way between lower lip and chin, which doesn't look true in most silhouettes. A collar, for boys can increase the appearance over a t-shirt. A cowlick, "rooster" or hair in disarray can be interesting and a lasting memory if a Mother wants it on the silhouette.

SKULL to CHIN equals **NOSE TIP to BACK of HEAD** which equals 4 times the **NOSE** length, with the ear being in the middle at 2 lengths of the **NOSE**.

ONE-EYE TEST - Close one eye. Hold the silhouette between you and the model. Move the silhouette to where you see the halo of the model's head around the silhouette. Only a snip or two on the silhouette may put everything in proportion. If the chin-line has changed with client's relaxation, hopefully it is thinner and you can snip a piece off. Facial features can change during a sitting, and if client likes it, don't worry. If the nose is larger, it can be trimmed. The tip of the lip may need snipping, particularly with children, to give it that necessary touch for "likeness."

Ending – Here's your chance to express your individuality in the way you finish your silhouette. Adopt some particular style and stick to it. Cut obliquely from the shoulder down and over to the start of the chest in a way that you want to be remembered. Autograph and date it.

Your practice cutting with patterns will probably be from white or brown Kraft paper (grocery sacks will do) and will not require mounting. When you have done a client, you will want to mat the silhouette and add your name or initials as well as the year of accomplishment.

Now, you've done it! Don't you feel you've made a good start?

Remember! Everything you need to know in order to cut the profile is right in front of your eyes. Give yourself a few days at this, or skip this procedure and practice the patterns that follow. After you have used them, you will see and grasp the meaning of the proportions.

A "quickie" way to get into silhouette cutting which gives you practice and encourages you to really get started is to take profile pictures, shoulder to head, xerox them to miniature size, place black paper behind them and cut the picture UP. It's opposite of sketch-ing where the pencil sketches down. You can also use this method to establish a mail order business, and cut silhouettes of people who can't sit for you. *This was the beginning of my becoming a Professional Cutter as I could not find anyone to teach me.* Soon, you will learn free-hand sillhouette cutting and can throw away all the props.

Regardless of the method used, the simplicity and dream-like glow of the ordinary silhouette cut from a piece of paper holds a special attraction. Surprises await the person who starts this journey from a black piece of paper and produces the most modest of pictorial arts. This is part of a family whose ancestors existed before recorded history and even emerged into our modern film-making techniques. Its romantic involvement dates back to Pliney the Elder, 600 B.C., when Corinthea drew the shadow of her departing lover on the wall. We think of the silhouette for a Valentine. Was that the first Val-entine?

Cutting By Pattern:

We merely give you copies of our silhouettes in various age groups to develop techniques, improve your skills, and use in a pinch "when all else fails." Don't say you can't do a silhouette when you have all these patterns before you.

Remember, as you look at a profile, God did not throw away the pattern. There are many people who look alike in profile, but never tell that to a Mother who thinks there is nobody like her child. She expects his individual profile to look different. It may be different from any of these patterns, but as you cut, you will see the difference and alter the tissue pattern accordingly, The main reason for these patterns is to quickly point out the proportions of profiles at various age levels. They can also be used when you have lines of people waiting, particularly if you have impatient Mothers or wiggly children.

While client is sitting in chair and deciding how many silhouettes to have, use procedure outlined on page 54-C. It is never noticed unless someone stands behind you to observe. Do not let this happen. To avoid injury with your swinging scissors, advise them that they can observe the procedure better in front of you, by looking at the client and you beyond, and seeing how the profile takes shape. (If a photographer wants a picture of you in action, insert another silhouette sheet in your hand, with black facing toward him and ask him to wait until you are about half through cutting to snap the picture. Then, the black silhouette can show in the photo, along with the child's face, as shown by the author on page 25.

Keep in mind the proportions and it will not be long before you are cutting adult heads without difficulty. It will take longer to learn to cut a child's profile to bring out his age. Children's heads come in many different shapes at different ages, but the pattern will usually fit, with a few snips here and there, at a given age.

The profile of the face will be no problem, especially if you use the pattern. The female's hair covers the head and avoids the dilemna over the bone structure of the back of the head.

On the male, what you see is not always what you want to put down, particularly if he has a short haircut. On black paper, it can look terrible. This is why a collar is often used to break up the neck line.

Study the sample patterns on pages 55 - 73 as you read the following:

The 1 year old's head is large with chubby, full cheeks and eyes lower on head. The chin and nose are quite small and lips often protrude as far as nose and chin. The neck is short and fat. (If the baby is dainty and thin, use the smaller pattern and alter accordingly.)

The older the child becomes, the head is smaller and neck is longer. The chin is more pronounced and mouth and nose are definitely shaped.

By the time a boy is 11, his head is much smaller, but the face has lengthened and is showing signs of maturity. The eyebrow line is about midway between the chin and skull line, and his neck is longer and thicker, Adam's apple starts to appear, jaw and chin become

44

quite definite, nose is longer but the tip is still up, and the nose bridge and brow bulge more prominently.

About the age of 20, man's head and nape of neck are heavier, mouth and jaw more firm, nose tips less and bridge deeper.

At age 40, neck could be heavier, second chin developing, fleshy roll at nape, mouth, more reserved, nose possibly longer, and hairline receeding.

At age 60, the neck, chin and jaws may sag. Baldness and bony features of skull may appear. Some profiles do not reveal age since wrinkles do not show.

Usually, for mature faces, good way to judge the proportions of the silhouette you are cutting, is to take 3 fingers and place them horizontally on the cutting with the forefinger covering from chin to nostril, the second finger from nostril to eyebrow and third finger from eyebrows to skull line. The 3 fingers can scan the distance vertically between the nose and back of skull. (page 41).

Increasing stages of development bring character that is easily expressed in profile, making it more recognizable in adults. However, if you cut a silhouette that makes a person look older, particularly children, you may have to re-cut the chin and pull it in. (Judge distance in by imagining a perpendicular line from nose to ground.)

Making Sample Copies of Patterns: (p. 55)

1.   Place stiff plastic (texture of a page-protector) over our samples, trace with pen from chest to top center of head, then from shoulder **up** in back to top. (This trains you to think **up** instead of down, opposite of what a portrait artist does.)   Cut plastics pattern in same manner. (Not with silhouette scissors.) This makes your permanent pattern for reuse, instead of ruining your book.

2.   Tissue/carbon (sold at office supply for typewriter copy) has better texture than regular tissue paper. Place plastic pattern over 3 sets, (a) outline with pencil, jerk carbon out, cut tissue in blocks, (b) place in pockets, (c) with nose to R, in same order as sample silhouettes in book.

3.   At the beginning, when you have traced samples, you may find it more convenient to distribute individual patterns between leaves in a book with labels dividing the pages. For example, "baby", "3 years", "boy 5 years", etc.

For Practice Cutting, Use This Procedure:

Tissue copy sample placed on white side of sihouette paper.

If samples are in a book or standing in a box (cata-
logued as to age) a quick procedure for cutting is as follows: dominate hand picks up silhouette paper and with
other hand folds black side together, places sample on
top of folded paper, ready to cut while client becomes
adjusted in chair and number of copies of silhouettes is

determined. If more copies are desired, tuck additional folded sheets between those in hand.

Now, you are ready to begin cutting silhouettes. If you are **Right-Handed, Subject should be facing parallel to your right shoulder** about 3 feet in front of you. Fold silhouette paper looking at white side. (Never cut on the black side of silhouette paper.) Hold silhouette paper in your left hand, feed it into the "hilt" of the scissors attached to right thumb and forefinger, and cut **UP** from the right lower corner of paper with the scissors, as shown in example. Don't "chew" with the scissors. Scissors should be held upright and not leaning R or L. After the cut, stop to re-adjust the paper to the "hilt" of the scissors, not like "snipping" the paper as is done with Scherenschnitte. You feed the paper into the scissors.

If you are **Left Handed, Subject should be facing parallel to your left shoulder.** You begin cutting **UP** from the lower left corner with your left hand, first, the chest, then the chin, lips, nose, eyelash, forehead, on to the top of the head, then flip the silhouette over and cut the back **UP** (just the reverse of what a right-handed person would do.) Next, you give it the "one eye" treatment by closing one eye, (holding the silhouette at eye level, between you and the client, at a few inches distant), and adjust it to where you see the outline of the silhouette parallel with the client's profile. If it isn't thus so, snip the silhouette at places where it will conform to the near likeness. After relaxing, patient may show a difference in the chin, pucker of the mouth, etc. It merely takes a snip to change it for the better.

Adhesive

Ready to glue? This is a *quick procedure* for mounting silhouettes - have several thicknesses of news-paper, cut in 5" squares and staple them together. Place each black face down on a square, paint a narrow strip of glue in a ring-around fashion (as shown on the example below, and place a dot of glue in center, as you hold on to the brush or a ***Popsicle Stick*** which is also practical. Flip it over on the mat in the proper place and smooth the face with the other hand. Give it and the subject the "óne eye treatment", sign and date it and slip it in envelope.

After mounting and signing your name, hold the finished product for clients and audience to view. If they have a puzzled look, tell them that you cut at "eye-level" and this is what you see. When it is framed and hung on the wall, you will see the "like-ness" – not as a picture, but as a "shadow."

If you've cut small details, such as wisps of hair, mustache, etc., tell them to slightly cup mat as it is slid into frame so these details will not tear.

Some silhouette artists use wall paper paste, but no glue is as good as rubber cement. If you are cutting many silhouettes, buy a large bottle of rubber cement and place a small quantity in a smaller jar, using a brush or a wooden popsicle stick to spread it on the paper and to hold the paper as you flip it over. If there are just a few clients waiting, a Glue Stick is ideal. With either one, it is necessary to cap the container as the glue dries quickly. Have a thinner nearby in case glue becomes too thick.

Erasure: Paint a strip of rubber cement on waste paper, let it dry and roll it into a ball. This can be used to pick off any glue on the face of the silhouette after it has dried a second. (Glue was my worst enemy until I learned this trick.)

Keep a damp cloth to wipe sticky fingers and black face of the silhouette if any speck or scratch shows up.

Stamp or Stickers: Name, address, phone number plus "For extra copies."

Tissue Copy/Carbon: Ream available at office supply.

Clipboard: Holds tissue when outlining patterns.

Pencil: To outline patterns, etc.

Pens: Fine-point permanent ink, for autograph. *Optional:* Calligraphy pen to sign clients name on mat. Silver-point pen for embellishing silhouette in lieu of cut-outs on profile. These features take time when clients are waiting, but good to keep a client in chair to attract customers.

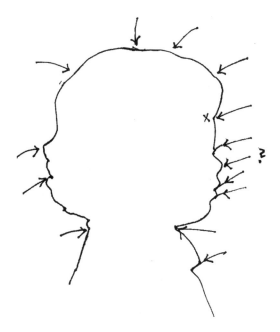

The length of the scissors and size of the silhouette determines where stops will be made with the scissor cut. In this sample, using 1 ½" blade, the arrows point to stops that are handy for pausing to view client. When you cut to the stops at the mouth, the nose (sometimes, depending on its length) and to the tip of the eyelash ¼". That will give you an anchor to begin the next cut at the pattern line. The shape of the hairdo will determine the stops at back of the head.

Making And Using Pockets To Hold Samples:

(a)

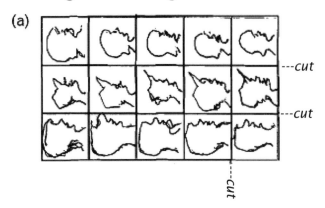

---cut

---cut

cut

B. Back to insert samples.

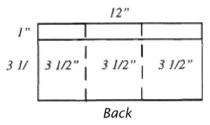

12"

1"

3 1/ | 3 1/2" | 3 1/2" | 3 1/2"

Back

Cut cardboard 4 ½" x 12". Fold beige plastic over cardboard and meet in back 1" from top. Stitch three, 3-1/2" pockets. Insert the plas tic sample and tissues behind, with nose facing R, in age sequence, leave top of head ½" outside.

C. With front facing you, black silhouette thereon and identical plastic sample and tissues in pocket behind it, you can insert R forefinger to slide tissue out and place over folded paper to cut. (Stretch mouth of pocket and cut ¼" moonshape in each for finger's easy access.) Familiarizing yourself with location of each sample helps you to work more rapidly.

Front

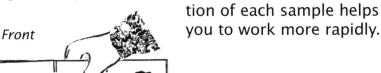

Sample silhouettes (these can be xeroxed):

54

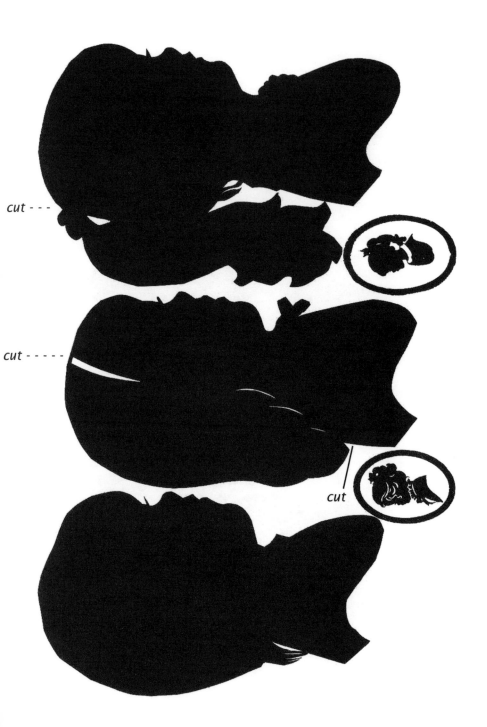

cut - - -

cut - - - - -

cut

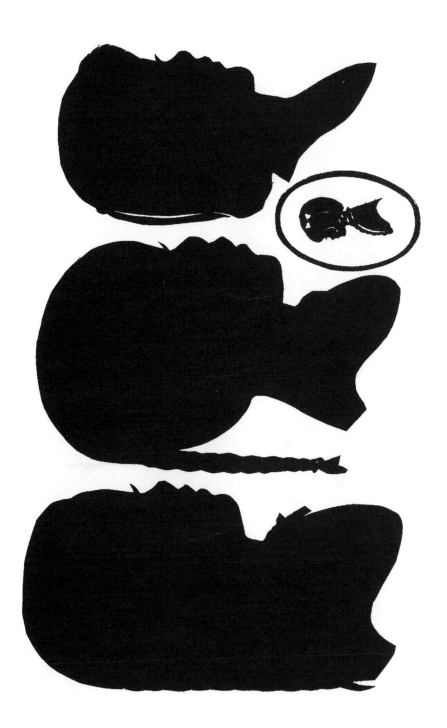

cut - - - - -

cut
/

cut - - - - -

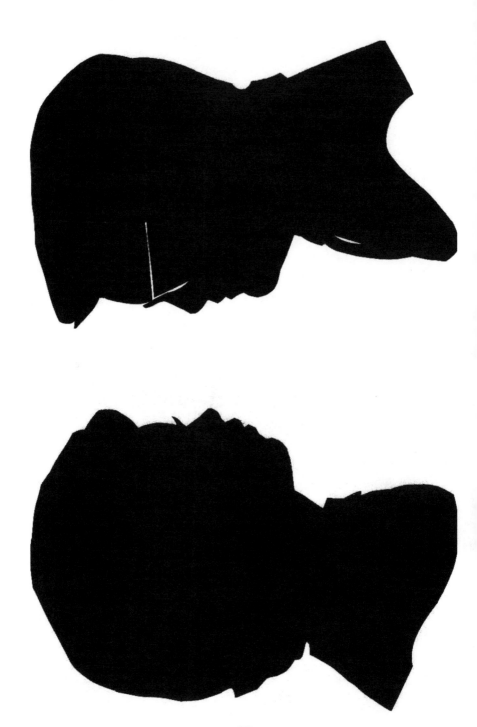

cut - - - - -

69

Doing Scenes and Things

Tape clear plastic wrap to framed glass you are holding in front of an object, person, or scene. (If it is a view you want from a window, tape the plastic wrap to the appropriate location on the window pane.)

With felt-tip pen outline what you want with the white side of the silhouette paper. Remove and roll the white side showing on the tube. Unroll on the board as you cut the intricate designs. It will keep your pattern and paper in good shape. Presto! You have, in proportion, what it takes an artist some time to sketch.

TRACING ON GLASS

Special Requests:

1.   A single copy - only if you want practice or to draw more customers. It takes as much time as cutting two copies, and after they have seen one, they usually ask for a second (which you'd have to do by outlining the first one and duplicating it.)

2.   Double silhouette. (See page 54 and 55). This is done by having an extra copy (with white side facing you) of the top profile. In matting, the white copy is slid forward and glued between the top profile and the accompanying profile, giving the appearance that the white is a line dividing the two faces. With this approach, the back of one head will be covered. If it is a Mother and a baby it is attractive but with 2 children it is best to have individual pictures that can be placed on the same mat, either facing each other or looking the same direction. That way there is a whole profile of each which gives better identity. if they still insist on a "double", suggest that they have one double and one single of each.

3.   Cutting triple: This is done in the same manner. Be sure to cut enough extra copies to allow for the white face to form a dividing line. Each time, charge for each additional sheet of silhouette paper. Three thicknesses cut fine, but more should be cut from the first outline. (Mats larger than 5" x 7" should be reserved for this use.)

4.   A family of silhouettes: You can offer a special price for this. Silhouettes may be arranged in a circle on a larger mat; lengthwise, with noses in same direction; with parents viewing children; or some other arrange-

ment, depending on the size of family.

5.   Full figure: this takes longer and is requested mostly for children. There are some samples herein. Price 2/3rd more.

6.   An older woman may want you to lessen her chin or straighten her nose, in a silhouette. Kidding you say, "You mean you want me to take off what it took you 35 years to put on?" You can add: "Don't worry, I'll make you look as if you came to me long ago."

7.   Don't be bashful in asking people as they pass by, at craft shows, if they'd like a silhouette. (This can't be done at shopping malls.) Crowds don't always notice one booth when there are a great number of crafters. They are not offended when you call their attention to what you are doing. Actually, many become clients because you have done this. Be Aggressive!

8.   Request, by phone or letter, for more copies of a silhouette. Suggest they send a copy or the original for you to duplicate. Then make the outline on the silhouette paper for duplication.

9.   **Lap children:** Can be held on a lap with both people facing to the right. If child is strapped on the parent's back, stand up and cut at "eye level." If in a stroller, you may have to kneel down to capture the likeness. (This can attract attention and bring more customers.) Don't hesitate to use a tissue pattern for children. You can slip it on the silhouette paper and remove it with the scraps of the silhouette while Mother is attending the child, deciding on how many copies, etc. She is so anxious to have the silhouette and when

you've done it she will love it forever. She will probably comment: "I don't see how on earth you ever did that" when she sees the magic of your scissors. Of course that's your secret.

10.   **Wiggly children:** Give them a minute to relax. If Mother says, "straighten up", "don't do like that," etc., ask her to ignore child for a moment. Tell him to sit back in the folding chair, put his feet on the top step, his hands on his knees, and let you know what he sees straight ahead.

If you are at school, have a picture on the wall that offers interesting questions for him to ponder. (I use a large Disney World Map. This really fascinates a child.)

Overcoming Difficulties:

Working conditions: Picture yourself at a summer festival, or at an OCTOBERFEST, with the possibility of wind or rain. Take all the necessary equipment for comfort and protection for self and supplies.

Location: If outdoors, try to get the best location possible for exposure. If indoors, your special request should be to set-up against the wall so you can display your advertising. Hopefully, you will have good lighting. If daytime, try to set-up near a window for outside light.

Price: Don't underprice! This varies with location. Choose more-affluent areas when possible. Never let any one try to reduce your price by bargaining. Let them know that they apparently don't appreciate the value of a silhouette. (You are treated with such respect and awe that this seldom happens.)

Occupational Hazards: A normal day's cutting, with pauses between customers, is no more strenuous than cutting a dress pattern, even when you net as much as $1,000. Any wide publicity should read, "Appointments suggested because of demand", and your sponsor should schedule one every 10 minutes. If you have a helper to paste and accept money, you can do a person in 3 to 5 minutes.

When you are without a customer, make a silhouette of your helper. An occupied chair is an attention getter.

Guarantee: If Mother says, "That doesn't look like my child," explain that you cut at eye level, which Mother's seldom notice until they are "grown and gone". Ask the Mother to bend down and look at the child as you have done, to compare the likeness. Advise that silhouettes are not supposed to say the same things as pictures, nor are they to be viewed closely. They are to send their mystic memories from a distance, just as a shadow. If all this fails to convince the client, do not charge her for cutting. Reply that a silhouette is to be a memory through the years and you would not want anyone to have a silhouette which would not serve that purpose.

If the child is old enough to understand, have fun with him. Tell him you don't want to give him a double chin or pointed head, talk about silhouettes, what he likes to do, or something funny. His silhouette will be done before he knows it. At the last you can say, "See that halo around his head?" and "Mother probably didn't know he had a halo."

A small child's interest can also be held by some one standing in front of him with a picture book, at his eye-level.

Having Doubts About Your Work?

Work quickly. Don't let a customer know there is any problem in cutting his silhouette. Rapidity of workmanship, which is emphasized in your advertising, makes for a better likeness. It is that quick glance, in the beginning, that registers in cutting. If you are using a pattern, the secret is to recognize the profile and the pattern that can be altered to create the likeness.

From the time you begin cutting until you finish, a client's profile can change, as he relaxes. As you hold the silhouette at "eye level" and adjust it in front of his profile, you may need to "snip" and alter the silhouette to create the likeness.

When you give the silhouette to the client, tuck a sheet of paper in the envelope indicating that "the silhouette is cut at eye-level. Also that the French silhouette paper is easily scratched and should be placed under glass as soon as possible. When it is framed and hung on the wall, it will come alive and people can easily recognize the "likeness."

Money Making Strategies:

1. Make silhouettes from black or colored contact paper and place on tiles, box's, etc. (must lacquer tiles afterwards.)

2. Applique silhouettes on quilts, pillows, towels, etc.

3. Make, or have made, rubber stamps of reduced-size miniature silhouettes for seals on envelopes, letterheads, etc.

4. Cut scenes, signs, objects, name-plates, etc., in silhouette.

5. Obtain pattern books from **Dover Publishing Company**, 180 Varick Street, New York, NY 10013; TREE TOYS, Box 492, Hinsdale, IL 60521; (for Scherenschnitte Kits) check out local craft shops.

6. Schedule your work where many children will attend.

7. Hold classes for senior citizens, clubs, scouts, handicapped children, etc.

8

Supplies:

If you can't find them, contact **Profile Press**, 6051 Greenway Court, Manassas, VA 20112 or email: profilepress@comcast.net. Our website is: www.profilepress.org.

To begin, you don't need many supplies. It's amazing what you can do, just with paper, scissors and glue -- at little expense for the benefits you receive. A little determination will put you in such a frame of mind that hours of fun will pass quickly.

Paper: Imported French silhouette paper, matte finish, offers the "professional" look. Large quantities of flat sheets, size 20"x26" can be cut to size 4"x6 ½" (using a sheet folded this make 40 silhouettes) Large paper cutters, located at schoois and print shops can cut sets of 100 sheets that offer convenience for big events. (Before cutting the full size sheets, you may want to pull out a few sheets for making scenes and things, roll them up until needed).

If you use a large sheet, fold white side so it is 3 ¼" and cut a strip. For right handed cutters follow this technique - place the strip on the L side of your work table and snip off the height required for each profile. This paper scratches easily, so be careful with the black side. Gummed black labels are available for silhouettes, but are more expensive and thicker. Black contact paper is attractive and splendid for large scenes, but takes too much time to peel when customers are waiting. Black dull paper, 5" or 6" wide, in a roll, is more difficult to keep glued and stay flat.

Other medium-weight papers, such as hi-gloss, glow, chrome Kraft, construction and even brown paper cut clearly, but a white sheet should be placed in front of a dark paper to prevent eye strain. Most papers are more expensive than silhouette paper and do not offer the quality, beauty, or texture.

Mat Board: This is what brings the silhouette to life. Light beige or ivory gives it a more antique look; however some people choose white. Texture should be at least the stiffness of a card; otherwise, it may wrinkle when paste is applied. A board, size 23" x 25" at art supply stores, can provide 20 mats for 5"x7" frames.

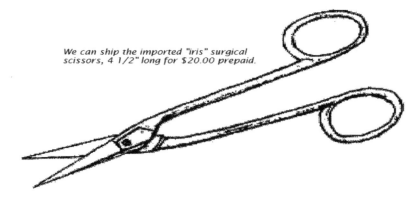

We can ship the imported "iris" surgical scissors, 4 1/2" long for $20.00 prepaid.

Scissors: Embroidery or other small, sharp, straight-blade scissors are OK, but "iris" surgical scissors, as above, blades 1" to 1½" that cut firmly from rivet to point are ideal. As many as 5 copies at a time can be cut without ragged edges, and these scissors seldom need sharpening. However, to test them, hold one ring of the handle, and if blade drops they need sharpening. Snip the corner off and if it cuts clearly, without tearing, scissors are OK. Run your fingers along blades, occasionally, to supply oil, or use oil drops sparingly.

Other Supplies you may want to have:

Frames: Oval frames give the traditional look, but rectangular frames, either in gold or black, look very nice. Some artists sell frames, but one should consider time wasted in putting it all together when other clients are waiting, the commission paid on sale, and the extra load of handling the frames.

Paper Bags: Buy from paper bag company in quantities, size preferably in yellow so they are not easily misplaced, or envelopes ready for mailing.

Rubber Stamp or Stickers: Used on back of mat with name, address, and phone number. This offers good advertising.

Tent: for inclement weather if you do craft shows.

Signs: Price list, and "I take wiggly children and grown-ups too."

Carrying Case for Patterns:

For your appointments, a book (as described on page ??) or a carrying case to hold your wallet, patterns standing up, scissors, glue stick, pen, and a small supply of silhouette paper and mats is very important. You have everything ready on a moment's notice. This can also be your "security blanket" until you have confidence. It comes in handy if you have a "squirming" child and Mother determined to get that silhouette. Your tools are on a table and the book or carrying case is in your lap. By sliding the tissue pattern out of the page or pocket, fold the silhouette paper with the tissue on top (page 53), ready to cut while child settles down. Then "snip" silhouette where needed when you hold it for the "one-eye test". A Mother often says: "I don't see how you managed to make the likeness." She's happy and only you know the "how."

You might be lucky enough to find a bag to carry all your supplies for an assignment, but I found a shoe-box the most ideal. A shoe box 5" tall x 14" wide can be made as follows:

1.   Take a black cloth, the width and length of shoe box, plus 1", and long enough to wrap around bottom long sides, over rim and to top center.

2.   Fold cloth over (making flaps) and run it to meet inside bottom center. Stitch ends together.

3.   Sew one flap, then the other with an open - end zipper to top of each flap to insure security from objects falling out.

4.   Insert cardboard stays to stiffen flaps.

5.   Attach a strap to complete the carrying case.

If you are doing a craft show, you will have to carry more than your carrying case. A tall beige plastic waste basket will hold a good many things such as extra mats, sample silhouettes, table cover, etc. This basket could be pulled on a luggage carrier, from your car to your spot.

Establishing A Market

1.	Request *Calendar of Events* from State Office of Tourism, Chamber of Commerce, Arts & Craft Guilds, etc.

2.	Check schedules of events listed in *Southern Living*, other magazines, and "What's Happening" in local newspapers. To get advanced information, locally, contact newspaper.

3.	Subscribe to **Sunshine Artist, 1700 Sunset Drive, Longwood, FL 32750.** (This magazine publicizes art and craft shows throughout the United States, giving details for participation and tips on effective promotions.)

4.	Contact Public Relations Offices of businesses, corporations, etc., for information on annual picnics, Christmas parties, and special promotional events (bank openings, store sales, etc.)

5.	Put ads in "Party" of local papers.

6.	Join a Craft Guild to participate in their shows and learn where others are being held.

7.	Visit craft shows, meet organizer to select most desireable location to work

8.	Place business cards or flyers (with sample silhouette thereon) on bulletin boards at art shops, grocery stores, etc. Screen calls for desireability.

9.   Contact church groups for Bazaars, Clubs, Girl Scout Troops, School Fairs, Cosmetic Salespersons and other organizations regarding "fund-raising" events.

10.   Start a club called the "Shady Ladies." You will have fun and if you are a "mobile" group, you will promote this almost-lost art in the far corners of the world.

Working at Schools

Telephone the director of the school, explaining that you are not a VIP except to Mothers who are desperately looking for someone to cut their children's silhouettes; that you'd like to come to their facility as a benefit to them (15% commission after sales tax is removed from price quoted); which is also a convenience to the Mother. Frankly, it is easier for you to have the child in a relaxed environment at school without Mother there, telling him to "straighten up."

You can assure the teacher you will have the silhouettes completed either the same day or next. If school pictures are scheduled soon, suggest that you arrange to do silhouettes the next season in order not to compete with the pictures.) Both Mothers and teacher often choose silhouettes over pictures because it often brings better results and an "antique quality" to remember. Pictures come and go, but everyone remembers a silhouette.

Inform the director that there is little to do on her part, since checks are made payable to you. She Xeroes your flyer for the parents, giving them a week to respond. You can then work out a schedule allowing 15 minutes for each child. Create a 3"x5" card for the event; add the cards mileage for your record. Take chair for child to be at "eye level", as well as picture to tape to the wall.

You are seated in a room away from the distractions of other children and the teacher sends the child to you with his envelope. While he is getting seated, you write his name, quantity desired and amount of check on his 6"x9" envelope or paper bag. Have the picture attached to the wall. Start asking him questions about the picture as you cut and suddenly you can show what you did with your "magic scissors." With some children it is best not to mention the word "cut." Once when a Mother suddenly saw us doing silhouettes, she said, "Come here Johnnie, we're going to have your silhouette cut." Johnnie didn't know what a silhouette was and you can imagine his reaction. Qualms can usually be dismissed when the subject is changed to the child's level, as your scissors dance around his silhouette and you talk about the picture on the wall.

After cutting, place silhouettes in bag, return them to classroom and take the next client. After all silhouettes have been cut, mount them, finish with your signature, and place in **Named** bag for delivery to teacher. You then total checks, deduct sales tax and give her a commission check.

Schedules for schools can be quite heavy so keep your calendar up-to-date and handy. You may have calls from Mothers asking questions on where more silhouettes can be cut. You've now created a market that has no end. Just wait until your client's profile is passed around for neighbors, friends and relatives to see. If you have placed your address sticker on the back of the mat your phone will be ringing. This continues year after year as a new brother, sister or cousin arrives. It takes only a look at a silhouette hanging on the wall for another Mother to envy and want to follow suit.

Sign For Schools

Dear Parents:

SILHOUETTES by _____ will be cut at our facility in a few days.

If you don't possess or own a silhouette this is an opportunity, a convenience, and a saving to have your child's miniature profile cut by this well-known artist, using a technique that is almost a dying art. This is a SPECIAL, unique and personal gift, not only for you - but for loved ones who will treasure it for generations to come.

_____ captivates children with her stories as she observes and cuts their likeness from French silhouette paper and places it on a antique ivory mat, ready for framing in five minutes. This can be done with even the "wiggly" children.

1. Write your child's name and number of desired copies on the face of an envelope.
2. Enclose cash or check payable to: _____
3. Return information within 5 days.

Prices include tax: $_____for 2 (1 for Grannie & I for You)
Extra copies available at $_____. each.

If you have further questions or wish to bring other children or friends to take advantaqe of this opportunity, please call_____ at _____ to make arrangements.

Be professionally organized and enthusiastic. Remember, you will be dealing with happy faces because you have something they want. Select your business card. Have a silhouette on it, plus: "Profile likeness hand-cut in 5 minutes at craft shows, fairs, marketing promotions, fund-raising events, or by appointment." In time, you may want a similar letterhead. You will need slides and photographs to show your display in applying for a juried show. Have samples, attractive signs and price list displayed at events.

Wearing a colonial costume (long skirt and blouse) attracts attention for this early-day craft/art and is often required. Watch calendar for paying bills, making appointments and meeting deadlines. You will want an answering machine so you won't miss any business.

Calendar:

This is very important. As invitations arrive, read carefully and note these features:

Date? Time? When to set-up? Cost? Are pictures and slides required for a juried show? Is the event well-publicized? Will children be there? Anticipated crowd? etc.

Evaluate the above factors and place in proper file: (1) Accept; (2) No; (3) Consider later (if nothing better). You learn from experience and from other crafters the best shows.

When you accept an invitation, if indoors, request to be near a window for sunlight, and wall space to hang samples of if outdoors, ask if it's possible to sit under a tree (unless you have a tent.) A silhouette artist is usually in a prominent space as the "star" of a show.

License Requirements:

County and city officials can advise you as it relates to where you are doing business. If you have a yearly or temporary vendor's license permit, it should be displayed when you participate in an event.

Taxes:

If it is required in your state, collect and indicate on sales receipt. Keep a copy for yourself for quarterly report to the State. You will need the State "seller's permit." (This also entitles you to buy supplies, without tax, for re-sale.)

Your copy of receipts to customers will substantiate your earnings and amount of tax you collected. Use the 3x5 card to show your expenditures for space, commissions and mileage at each event. (Your 15% commission check, eliminates receipts at school.)

Retirement Plans:

Contact bank, fund or stock broker to obtain forms for Keogh & IRA contributions as a deduction. You provide information for social security credits on Schedule C of Federal Form 1040.

Keeping Records:

Internal Revenue Service requires it and you need the information to receive benefits toward retirement plans. Customize your own ledger columns, running horizontally, as follows:

Expenditures:

Date and Check payable: Open a bank account solely for this purpose. Never use for personal expense. If you pay yourself, designate "withdrawal."

Advertising: Newspapers, flyers, letters, etc.

Car Expense: Record odometer readings each time used. Count small repairs.

Commission: Percentage or space-rental.

Dues & Publications: Local paper and craft publications featuring events.

Office Expense: Miscellaneous items, postage.

Supplies: Silhouette paper, carbon copy paper, mats, glue, scissors, pens, pencils, bags, etc.

Travel Expense: Lodging, taxi, tips, etc., business entertainment but not food.

Phone calls: Business.

Place expense receipts in envelopes named for the above categories and record monthly in **Ledger**. Refer to current Federal and State Laws.

Conducting business in your home may qualify you for income tax deduction. This would necessitate your keeping records of certain expenses relating thereto.

Your Display Booth:

Keep your work desk as uncluttered as possible. A card table is ideal. Have a cover that touches the floor and keep excess supplies, etc., beneath. Set up with a strip of heavy duty absorbent paper toweling across the table. A clip board is handy for holding mats and newspaper squares to place silhouettes on for glueing. Pin plastic bag to corner of table for trash. Keep a wet paper handy to wipe glue from fingers.

A chrome portable coat rack (easily disassembled) is ideal for displaying behind you samples of your silhouettes. After assembling the rack, you can drop a bright solid cover over it to hang your signs and sample silhouettes. Place sample silhouettes on large mat board and cover with clear plastic in lieu of glass.

Attach a long string of twine to several samples and pin at intervals between samples on top of display rack, on the edge of your table, umbrella stand, etc. for advertising. Buy 1/2" black contact tape and make borders on samples to give them a framed look. They fold easily for packing and eliminate the hazards of glass.

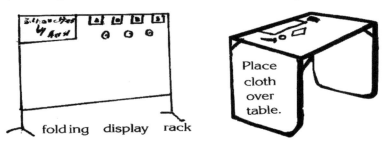

folding display rack

Place cloth over table.

Clever signs could be as follows:

Think Christmas!!
*Surprise Someone With
A Silhouette.*

I take "wiggly" children and
grown-ups too!, also checks.

2 of 1 face - $_____
(1 for Grannie; 1 for you)
Extra's only $_____ each.

Hear _____,
Silhouette Artist,
relate the *History of Silhouettes* as she cuts miniature
profiles for 5"x7" mats and readies them for your
SPECIAL gift.

On the back of the folding step stool, a sign could
read: "Silhouettes in 5 minutes."

Pack Orderly and take note of supplies needed, when
you finish an assignment, so you can be ready for the
next, without delay. A beige plastic kitchen trash can
placed on a luggage cart looks neat and is practical for
supplies.

Afterward:

We wrote **Silhouette Cutting for Fun and Money** because of our desire to keep this art form of "miniature" silhouettes from becoming a lost art. You may find books on the history of silhouettes, but this has the only step-by-step method of how to cut silhouettes and how to market your trade.

In this book, we have endeavored to explain every possible situation that may confront you as you seek to prepare yourself for this new hobby and means of self- employment. However, there is one warning: Don't rush work on a client simply because there are others waiting. Concentrate solely on him and you will be rewarded. You want it to be exact likeness that will be admired by all who look upon it, and treasured for generations to come.

We've traveled many miles to gather information and have found few silhouette artists. This is our own technique to practice and learn S**ilhouette Cutting for Fun and Money** and many people have profited by it. How do we know? By the orders we have received for supplies and the many letters which indicate that our book has opened for them, a "brand new world."

Bibliography:

The major source for writing *Sillhouette Cutting for Fun and Money* comes from our first-hand experience and simple techniques we designed to teach ourselves. The following books offered no suggestions on how to cut silhouettes, but have a great deal of information on silhouette cutters and photographs of their work. These books can be found through **www.amazon.com** or your local bookstore.

Unlikely Silhouettes/NR by Mark Cdpope

The Art of Silhouette by Desmond Coke

Silhouettes, Collector's Pieces by Peggy Hickman, 1968

Two Centuries of Silhouettes by Peggy Hickman, 1971

Silhouettes, A Living Art by Peggy Hickman, 1985

Ancestors in Silhouette Cut, by August Edouart, by Emily Jackson, 1977

Silhouettes, A History and Dictionary of Artists, by E. Nevill Jackson

Auguste Edouart: A Quaker Album: American and English Duplicate Silhouettes 1827-1845 by Helen & Nel Laughton

British Silhouette Artists and their Works by Sue McKenzie

British Profile Miniaturists by Arthur Mayne

Artistic Silhouettes by M. Floyd Morris

Beauty in Black and White by Nellie Earles Quimby

Silhouettes in America, 1790-1840: A Collectors Guide by Blume J. Rifkin

Shades of our Ancestors, by Alice VanLeer Carrick, 1928

Miniatures and Silhouettes: Modes and Manners Supplement by Max Von Boehn

To All of Those interested in Papercutting!

As a result of widespread interest in papercutting, a papercutters' group was formed in 1988. It is "The Guild of American Papercutters" (GAP). The organization is specifically for those interested in the many forms of papercutting.

GAP was established for members from North America, Europe, Asia and Australia. Members range from amateurs to professionals; beginners to teachers, as well as those who do not cut but have an academic interest in papercuttings. Their accomplishments include 400 members located in 46 states and 11 countries, publish the quarterly magazine "First Cut", papercutting exhibits and programs at various museums, traveling exhibits of members' papercuttings in the United States, and gathering of North American papercutters at the bi-annual "Collection" since 1994.

Many GAP members get to know each other, share papercutting interest, creativity and styles, as well as artistic goals. If you are a cutter, or just interested in papercutting, and would like to know more about the Guild, you can visit their website at: **www.papercutters. org.**